BOOK OF

Thyme

BOOK OF
Thyme

JACKIE FRENCH

Angus&Robertson
An imprint of HarperCollins*Publishers*

AN ANGUS & ROBERTSON BOOK
An imprint of HarperCollinsPublishers

First published in Australia in 1993

CollinsAngus&Robertson Publishers Pty Limited
A division of HarperCollinsPublishers (Australia) Pty Limited
25 Ryde Road, Pymble NSW 2073, Australia

HarperCollinsPublishers (New Zealand) Limited
31 View Road, Glenfield, Auckland 10, New Zealand

HarperCollinsPublishers Limited
77–85 Fulham Palace Road, London W6 8JB, United Kingdom

Distributed in the United States of America by
HarperCollinsPublishers
10 East 53rd Street, New York NY 10022, USA

Copyright © Jackie French 1993

National Library of Australia
Cataloguing-in-Publication data:

French, Jacqueline.
  Book of thyme.
  ISBN 0 207 17855 0.
  1. Thymes. 2. Herb gardening. 3. Cookery (Herbs). I. Title
635.7

Printed in Hong Kong

  5 4 3 2 1
97 96 95 94 93

CONTENTS

THYME

WHERE THE WILD THYME BLOWS

I know a bank wheron the wild thyme blows,
Where oxlips and the nodding violet grows
Quite over-canopied with luscious woodbine,
With sweet musk-roses and with eglantine...

~

WILLIAM SHAKESPEARE, A MIDSUMMER NIGHT'S DREAM

Lovers have rolled on it; soldiers in ancient times grilled their meat over it; the Egyptians used it to preserve their dead; Alexander the Great may have used it to get rid of nits while on campaign. Cats like to squat by it, opera singers gargle with it, medieval aristocrats sniffed it to ward off the plague — thyme is one of the staple herbs, grown and experimented with for millennia, used medicinally, in magic spells, in cosmetics and, of course, as a culinary herb.

If I had to choose one single herb to grow fresh for cooking (which heaven forbid), it would be thyme. Thyme is the most adaptable of herbs. Used sparingly it brings out other flavours; used with more abandon it gives a richness and flavour of its own. It can be used fresh at any time of the year. Though dried thyme gives a good approximation of fresh thyme's qualities, it only conveys its strength without its subtlety. The only way you taste thyme's true flavour is to use it fresh, straight from the garden.

Growing herbs can become a passion — and thyme is no exception. Its uses are so varied and its fragrance so pungent (even a whiff of it evokes memories of my grandmother's roast shoulder of lamb, and the dripping she saved from it and kept in the refrigerator) that it is easy to conjure up its scent when wondering how to flavour a new dish. Kipling compared the scent of thyme to the perfume of the dawn in paradise.

Greek maidens wore garlands of thyme flowers in their hair in the belief that it would make them irresistible. (I haven't tried this so I don't know if it works!) Gourmets fed on the classic thyme honey from the wild thyme that grew on the slopes of Mount Hymettus.

Thyme was also used as a perfume by Greek and Roman men and one of the greatest compliments you could pay an ancient Greek warrior was to say he 'smelt of thyme' — it meant he was courageous, not vaguely smelling of last night's marinated octopus. Thyme is also one of the ingredients in herbal tobacco.

In the Middle Ages it was believed that sleeping on a pillow of thyme would dispel melancholy, or inspire knights to be courageous. There is a lovely medieval tale of a cowardly knight who slept on a bank of thyme and when he woke he was ready to do battle again.

Are you going to Scarborough fair,
(Parsley, sage, rosemary and thyme)
Remember me to one who lives there,
She once was a true love of mine...

~

TRADITIONAL

Marinated Feta Cheese

SERVES 4

~ 500 g (1 lb) feta cheese, cut in chunks

~ 1 cup (8 fl oz) olive oil

~ 10 black olives

~ 1 stalk celery, finely slivered

~ half a thinly sliced red capsicum (sweet pepper)

~ 20 sprigs fresh thyme — lemon, orange, caraway or plain thyme are suitable, though with varying effects

Mix all the ingredients together, place in jars and seal. Leave for at least 3 weeks before opening; or store for up to a year in a cool place.

Thyme is native to the Mediterranean region, where it is found on southern shores and northern hills, and in the Himalayas. It thrives in China, and even in Africa's Atlas Mountains and Ethiopia, and was known as far back as ancient Babylon (as were bay, saffron, cumin and juniper). Wherever it grows it is used: in tonics, medicine, and most of all in food.

Thyme is added to a great number of other foodstuffs, from cheese to fish to apples, from bread to various meats and tomato or potato dishes. It is hard to think of any other herb that is so versatile. Thyme is also used to flavour meat 'on the hoof' — lamb, goat, snails and mutton that have fed on hillsides of wild thyme have been prized for centuries, and in Italy herds of sheep are still sent to graze on pastures of thyme. The fragrant clumps of kitchen thyme most gardeners are familiar with is only one of about four hundred species of thyme — in fact, there are probably many more still unidentified varieties. Thyme hybridises readily, and the thyme above one valley may be quite different from the thyme on the opposite hill.

This multiplicity of species, many of which are superficially very similar, has also led to enormous confusion over the correct appellation of many of the species now cultivated and sold. Even named cultivars from nurseries may look suspiciously variable, and some sold under different names may be the same. When in doubt, taste and sniff.

Thyme was probably brought to Britain by the Romans, though it doesn't appear to have been generally grown till the sixteenth century. It was mostly grown as an annual, and in very cold areas some winter protection is still needed, though there appear to be more cold-hardy cultivars today.

Kitchen thyme was certainly in Australia by the early 1800s, and lemon thyme by the middle of the century. By 1860 thyme was popular in gardens and as a border plant for paths — low borders like thyme were needed, according to one garden writer, as higher borders might be damaged by crinolines sweeping past. Thyme was also used in a multitude of good British dishes, such as stuffed lamb.

No garden should be without...a few roots of Sage Thyme Mint Marjoram (sic) and other pot herbs; and these can be procured at any seed stores.

~

GEORGE SMITH, THE COTTAGE GARDENER, BALLARAT, 1862

A Medieval Recipe to Cure Shyness

To a mug of ale, add 13 sprigs of wild thyme. Stir with a red hot poker (don't use the microwave; you need solid iron for this). Drink hot. If a more sustaining drink is needed, break two raw eggs into the ale before the poker is inserted.

This may not cure shyness, but it will certainly provoke conversation.

Traditional Bouquet Garni

This is the classic addition to soups, stews and stockpots.

~ 2 sprigs parsley

~ 2 sprigs thyme

~ 1 sprig marjoram

~ half a bay leaf

Wrap the herbs in a small sachet and remove when the food is cooked. You can also tie them together with string and hope they don't disintegrate, or leave them floating in the pot for guests to pluck out as they munch.

Thyme Cheese

SERVES 4–8
*(depending on whether there
are other appetisers)*

*Beat ½ teaspoon salt into
4 cups (32 fl oz) natural
(plain) yoghurt. When it is
creamy, pour into a clean
teatowel or cheesecloth
(muslin) over a strainer.
Gather up the ends of the
teatowel and tie them together,
then hang it in a cool place. (I
hang mine from the bath tap,
so the whey drains into the
bath.) Leave for 48 hours.*

*Unwrap the curds and roll
them into small rounds, then
roll each round in fresh thyme
leaves. Place the rolled cheeses
in small jars and top with
olive oil. At this stage you can
add chopped dried tomato,
chillies, capsicums (sweet
peppers) or garlic to the oil.
Keep the cheese in the oil for at
least 3 weeks, though it can be
kept for months.*

THE HERB THAT GROWS
ITSELF

*For the sake of honey we have brought thyme out of Attica, but
there is great difficulty in raising it from seed...*

~

PLINY THE ELDER, ROMAN NATURALIST, (AD 23–79)

Thyme grows itself. After all, it is basically a wild
species, a perennial that will ramble up hills or
down banks without anyone to tend or water it.

Thyme has been called 'the poor man's herb'
because once you have a piece it will reward you
with no other outlay on your part.

In fact, most problems with thyme arise from too
much care — overwatering or overfeeding — or
by trying to grow it in areas that are too cold, too
wet, or too shady. Give thyme warmth, sun, and a
reasonably dry, well-drained, light soil, and it
will thrive.

Thyme prefers slightly limy soil, well drained,
with good sunlight, although I've grown thyme
successfully in very acid soil, and semi-shade.

However, thyme grown in semi-shade becomes
'leggy' and is prone to rotting and so has a much
shorter life than when grown in sunlight.

Don't feed your thyme; it doesn't need it. Too
much feeding produces a profusion of leaves but
they'll be less fragrant and more prone to disease.

Don't overwater either; thyme will survive in
almost dry soil. Remember that they are hillside
plants, springing up in dry shallow soils with
heat on their backs and on their leaves.

REVITALISING THYME BUSHES

Thyme will tolerate even the heaviest frost, except for older 'woody' plants that can be damaged in cold weather. Cut back older plants by three-quarters every year, and this problem should be eliminated.

Woody clumps may also progressively die back from the centre. If your thyme bush is very woody, or if it has been damaged by frost or an exhausting summer, revive it with a deep watering overnight followed by broadcasting moist soil over the stems. The bush will 'layer' itself by growing new roots from the stems and within a few months these new roots will stimulate new growth to cover up the bare patches in the middle of the bush.

It's a good idea to take cuttings of your thyme every few years and to replace old bushes, unless you can regularly prune them. I whippersnip our bank of thyme lightly every winter. It works well — except when I cut too deeply and kill the plant. Scissors are best.

INCREASING THE FRAGRANCE OF THYME

Thyme becomes more fragrant:
~ in mid to late summer when it is flowering
~ when grown in a hot climate
~ when grown on poor soil without excess nitrogen
~ if not given too much water
~ if kept in a sunny spot (in cool areas try a pot on the windowsill)
~ if grown, according to folklore, with camomile or parsley, though
from my own experience I've found no difference

It is easy to lose the fragrance of thyme, unless you can roll on it or
catch the scent in some other way. Ours grows in paving below a bank
of other herbs and on hot days the scent rises up the bank and floods the
air around the clothes line. Grow your thyme on the edge of a garden
where you often kneel, or by a path where you will brush against it, or
in a pot by the front door so the scent wafts inside in the afternoon sun.

PROPAGATING THYME

Thyme was traditionally planted on Good Friday (the day when evil was said to be absent) to ensure that it grew well.

Thyme grows either from seeds or cuttings. The latter is probably the best way to propagate thyme because cuttings grow faster than seedlings, and if you are growing several sorts of thyme it is possible that they will cross-pollinate.

(If you are adventurous, this may be an advantage, but I have to admit that after many years of sowing thyme seed — and growing about a dozen varieties — I have produced nothing but very small variations of the parent plants). It is also possible to divide many of the varieties, especially the matting forms.

Dividing Thyme

Using a sharp knife, cut a small piece of root and stalk. Plant in soil similar to the soil it was taken from, to minimise shock. Water well to settle it in, then keep fairly dry, as you would an established plant.

Herb Bread with Thyme and Sunflower Seeds

SERVES 4–6

~ 1 kg (2 lb) plain (all-purpose) flour
~ 1 sachet dried yeast
~ 1 tbspn fresh thyme, stalks removed
~ 1 tbspn finely chopped parsley
~ 1 tbspn celery seeds
~ 1 tbspn chopped sunflower seeds
~ 2 tbspns oil

Preheat oven to 200°C (400°F). Grease and flour a loaf pan. Combine all the ingredients and add enough water to make the flour damp, but not sticky. Knead as long as you can; the more you knead, the better the bread. Cover with a damp teatowel. Leave in a warm place till the dough doubles in size. Punch down and then knead again. Place in a grease pan, either as two loaves or as smaller rolls; brush with melted butter. Dust with more celery seed, poppy seed or sesame seed or leave plain. Cook in the preheated oven till the loaves or rolls shrink from the sides of the tin and are brown on top. (About 15 minutes for rolls or 30 minutes for loaves.)

Marinated Grape Leaves

❧

Layer fresh grape leaves in olive oil, interspersed with sprigs of fresh flowering thyme. Use the preserved, scented grape leaves in winter, wrapped round rice or ricotta or other soft cheese.

Fragrant Mushroom Soup with Lemon Thyme

❧

SERVES 2–4

~ *1 white onion, finely chopped*

~ *4 cloves garlic, chopped, not crushed*

~ *4 tbspns olive oil*

~ *3 cups mushrooms, very finely sliced*

~ *3 cups (24 fl oz) chicken stock (or water)*

~ *a dash of sherry*

~ *1 tspn fresh lemon thyme*

Sauté the onion and garlic in the olive oil. Add the remaining ingredients and simmer 5 minutes — no more. Serve hot or chilled.

TAKING CUTTINGS

Take cuttings of thyme bushes from old wood that 'snaps'. This is best done in moderately warm weather as cuttings tend to rot before they take if the weather is too cold.

Cuttings also take best if the plant is not in flower, though this isn't essential. The cutting can be a snip off an old branch (bits closest to the soil take best) or have a heel, that is, a part of the main stem. Cuttings with a heel take best, but you may not be able to find a suitable piece. Most cuttings will take anyway.

Place your cuttings in moist soil in semi-shade. Don't transplant them for at least six months, even if they seem to be growing well. Wait for good roots to develop. Don't put cuttings in full sunlight until new roots have formed. Be warned: thyme will stay fresh for weeks in a jar of water, or in moist soil, without any root development at all.

GROWING THYME FROM SEED

Thyme seed is difficult to collect — it is very small and is ready over a long period of time so it's easy to miss most of it. It is best collected by tying pieces of old nylon stocking over the flower heads once the petals have fallen. Or you can just take a chance and run your fingers up the stalks when you think the seeds are dry.

Store seed in an old envelope — not in plastic or foil or it may rot. Use a few lavender flowers or drops of lavender oil or dried bay leaves to keep weevils away.

Sow thyme seed in moist but not wet soil, and cover it very lightly. Seed planted too deeply will rot. An alternative is to scatter the seeds along narrow furrows scored by an old garden fork — as soon as you water them the furrows will gently close over the seeds, covering them shallowly.

Thyme seeds germinate in three to four weeks at 21°C (70°F), though they germinate quite well with daytime temperatures as low as 15°C (60°F). You can also 'pre-germinate' thyme seed by wrapping it in a wet towel and putting the towel in a plastic bag. Check for sprouting every day, then plant the seeds as soon as a few have sprouted.

Keep young thyme plants well watered and away from very strong sunlight until they are well risen from the soil. When they are about half the size of your thumb, plant them about 30 cm (13 in) apart, or closer if you want a 'hedge' or a quick carpet.

Carrot and Thyme Timbale

SERVES 4

~ 500 g (1 lb) carrots

~ ½ cup (4 fl oz) sour (soured) cream

~ 3 eggs, lightly beaten

~ a scattering of fresh thyme leaves

Boil and mash the carrots. Mix in the sour cream, eggs and thyme. Fill into small buttered pots (mousse pots are ideal) and place in a baking dish of water. Cook in a moderate oven (190°C/375°F) until firm. The time taken will depend on the size of the pots, probably about 20 minutes. Unmould, and serve hot.

TO MAKE A THYME LAWN

But those which perfume the air most delightfully, not passed by as the rest, but being trodden apon and crushed, are three: that is burnet, wild thyme, and watermints. Therefore you are to set whole alleys of them, to have the pleasure when you walk or tread.

~

SIR FRANCIS BACON, ESSAYS (1516–1626).
(Bacon was an enthusiastic gardener as well as Chancellor of England).

Thyme lawns are hardy, drought resistant, need very little (if any) watering, need no fertilising, and never need mowing. Bees love them, children love them (they are wonderful to roll on), and cats will go into an ecstasy of rolling and scratching. They are the perfect lawn for anyone who doesn't want to spend their weekends mowing and their evenings watering. Their major drawback is that they cost more and are more difficult to establish than grass lawns — especially if you plan to simply wait till grass seed blows in from your neighbours, and mow till it turns into lawn.

16
~

You must use matting thymes for lawns, that is, small-leaved varieties that spread rapidly, instead of clumping. You can either grow one form of thyme, or mix several, so that you will have either a carpet of one colour in summer when it flowers, or a patchwork. Since most thymes don't flower at exactly the same time there is usually some overlap, so for the most spectacular effect over a long time stick to one sort.

Thyme lawns can be grown from cuttings, or plants bought at the nursery, but by far the cheapest way is to buy lawn thyme seed. Make sure it is lawn thyme seed you are buying — a large expanse of clumps of culinary thyme may look pretty but will be awkward to walk on. Choose an area that gets full sun, is well drained and has light or sandy soil. A little lime added before planting may help, but unless the soil in your garden is very acid the thyme will survive without it.

Tapenade

SERVES 4–8
(depending on whether you serve other appetisers as well)

~ 2 tbspns capers

~ 4 anchovies

~ 1 tsp fresh thyme

~ 2 tbspns olive oil

~ 1 cup (5 oz) black olives, stoned

Blend the capers, anchovies, thyme and olive oil. Add the olives and blend again till coarsely mixed. Serve as an hors-d'oeuvre on very fresh bread, hot unbuttered toast or poppy seed crackers.

Thyme seeds can be sown at any warm time of the year but lawns are best sown in spring to early summer so they have a chance to become established before winter. Otherwise weeds may encroach on the bare ground.

All areas that you plan to put under thyme should be weed free. It is very hard to weed thyme lawns and almost impossible to get grass out of them, unless you resort to selective grass-killing herbicides.

First remove all grass and weeds. Rake the soil lightly, then cover with clear plastic. This will encourage the remaining weed and grass seeds to germinate. Wait three weeks, and rake again. (There is no need to dig the soil deeply before planting thyme seeds, the thyme roots will do all the digging necessary.)

Thyme seeds are very small. Mix them with four parts of dry sand and sprinkle them across the bare ground. If you sprinkle them unmixed, they tend to clump. Now sprinkle on some dry soil, or more sand. Keep moist until the thyme plants show half a dozen leaves or more, then gradually ease off the watering.

Restrain yourself from fertilising. The plants may grow faster initially but they will be more prone to disease and the last thing you want is bare brown patches in your thyme lawn. If this happens, trim the affected plants — or pull out dead ones — and drizzle the whole area with camomile tea. Replant with cuttings from unaffected patches.

If your thyme lawn shows signs of losing its vigour, sprinkle a bag of potting mix lightly over the lawn. Repeat the treatment the following week and again the week after. New roots will start to grow on the old bare stalks.

As thyme lawns are not mown and there are no clippings removed, they rarely need fertilising. The 'top dressing' of potting mix should be enough to revitalise a flagging lawn.

WHERE TO GROW A THYME LAWN:

~ instead of grass in a small courtyard

~ between paving stones

~ to cover a mounded rockery (use several different varieties of thyme here)

~ under a bed of rugosa roses that don't need much watering

~ as paths edged by bricks or stone

~ between the concrete or paved strips of a driveway

~ down a bank too steep to mow

~ under a clothes line (to avoid having to mow)

~ in paths through your vegetable and flower garden

~ to replace your main lawn — though the thyme lawn should be edged with sleepers and the like to keep grass from encroaching. As you don't need to mow a thyme lawn, you can scatter boulders or paving stones through it to break up the boring flatness of most lawns.

Grilled Thyme Prawns (Shrimps)

SERVES 4

~ 1 kg (2 lb) prawns, peeled but not beheaded

~ 1 cup (8 fl oz) olive oil

~ 2 chillies, chopped

~ juice of 2 limes (or lemons, if you must)

~ grated zest of 1 lime or ½ a lemon (or ½ cup chopped fresh lemon grass leaves)

~ 1 tbspn fresh lemon thyme, or plain thyme

Mix all the ingredients together. Leave to marinate in a cool place for 2 hours, then grill (broil) the prawns. Unfortunately the marinade can't be used again as the prawns may have contaminated it. Feed it to the hens to increase their egg production. Serve as an appetiser or main course.

OTHER WAYS OF GROWING THYME

*The success of this recipe
depends on how well you can
poach eggs. Break FRESH
eggs into a little simmering
water (the white of stale eggs
spreads; fresh egg white holds
together, resulting in a neater
poached egg). Scoop out each
egg with a slotted spoon when
the white is just set but the
yolk is still very runny.*

*Now heat ½ a cup (4 fl oz)
chicken stock for every egg. If
it is good, home-made stock
will turn into jelly by itself; if
you are dubious, add a
teaspoon of gelatine dissolved
in a little water for every
½ cup of stock. At the last
minute add ½ a teaspoon of
fresh thyme per egg — don't
let the thyme cook in the stock
or it will spoil the flavour and
appearance. Place the poached
egg in a small container — a
mousse pot is ideal. Cover with
the warm stock and cool till
set.*

*These eggs are delightful —
as you break into them the
yolk runs through the herb
and chicken jelly, and is
delicious.*

THYME IN A POT

Thyme can be grown in a pot on the windowsill,
as long as it is a very sunny windowsill, and you
force yourself not to water it every time you water
your maidenhair fern. Most pots of thyme die
from too much love, not too little. Fill the pot
with half sand and half potting mix, with a little
charcoal at the bottom to help keep the mixture
sweet.

If the plant turns 'leggy', with long stems and
very few leaves all turning towards the sunlight,
you will know the plant isn't getting enough sun.
Find another place for it. (I'm sure there must be
a medieval curse somewhere on people who
misuse their thyme plants — though I haven't
found it yet.)

Herb Wheel

Thyme is irreplaceable in the old-fashioned 'herb wheel'. You can use an old bicycle wheel to delineate your garden spacing (in past years an old wagon wheel was used). Use thyme as an edging plant, all around the rim, with the taller plants behind. It can also be used along each 'spoke', to separate the other herbs. In the spokes plant savory, matting rosemary, parsley, tarragon, garlic in autumn and winter followed by basil, chives, sage, marjoram and lovage — one herb to each spoke.

Thyme Courtyard

I love paving — it doesn't need mowing or weeding and the children can ride their skateboards over it with impunity. You can break up unrelieved paving by taking out every fourth paver and planting a herb like thyme. This way you get greenery without the weeds. Thyme loves the dry heat of paving — and most matting thymes are hardy enough to tolerate a bit of skateboarding as well.

An alternative is to use paving blocks with holes in them, specially prepared for planting — or the bricks with holes (these are used in walls where electric wiring is to be inserted).

A Thyme Wall

An old-fashioned favourite, this is a low stone wall with the top filled in with soil and thyme planted along it. Thyme tolerates both heat and fairly dry soil, and unlike many other plants doesn't have invasive roots to tear the wall apart.

Thyme Edges

Clumps of thyme make a lovely edging for a path or driveway. Use clumping rather than matting thyme, and trim lightly every winter to keep the 'hedge' shape and to stop the bushes becoming woody.

Mock Chicken

❦

4 SMALL OR 2 LARGE SERVES

These are excellent; far better than bubble and squeak or hash browns for breakfast.

~ *500 g (1 lb) carrot, grated*

~ *500 g (1 lb) potatoes, grated*

~ *1 tbspn fresh thyme*

~ *1 tbspn plain (all-purpose) flour*

~ *2 eggs, lightly beaten*

~ *butter or olive oil for frying*

Mix all the ingredients together. Place small spoonfuls of the mixture in a hot pan with lots of butter, or a combination of half butter and half olive oil. Fry one side till well browned then flip over and brown the other side. Serve hot. Each spoonful should be small, or the raw potato and carrot may not cook properly. If the mixture sticks to the pan, the oil is probably not hot enough.

A THYME SEAT

Popular in Elizabethan times, a stone seat was hollowed out and planted with thyme. You can make your own by filling a large concrete planter box with good soil mixed with sand and planting it out with any of the 'matting' thymes, then supporting it either on a pile of bricks or paving stones, or logs etc.

Thyme seats are wonderful to sit on on summer evenings, or sunny winter mornings — the heat brings out the scent of thyme and they feel warm and soft. Beware of thyme seats in summer, though — bees love them too.

A THYME TOWER

Buy a tall 'herb' pot with openings down the side, or simply take a large can, paint it white and cut holes down its sides, turning the sharp edges in to avoid injuring passers-by. Fill with half sand, half potting mix and plant clumps of thyme at the top and in every hole. They will gradually spill downwards, making a 'wall' of thyme. This form of cultivation suits thyme, but many herbs can't tolerate heat on their roots and the dryness of a tall pot.

If you use a painted can, you can nail it to a post or a wall.

A THYME WISHING WELL

Wishing wells are dangerous unless barricaded — children, cats and birds fall into them. They also breed mosquitoes, and much of our groundwater nowadays is contaminated. If you decide to build a wishing well anyway, fill it with rocks then top with any loam. Plant it with thyme, both green and silver varieties, to look like flashing water.

A HERB CHEQUER BOARD

This is the same principle as the herb wheel except that it has squares instead of spokes. Again, thyme is ideal as an edging for each square — it is perennial and doesn't die down in winter, unlike parsley or basil; it doesn't spread like marjoram or mint, and thyme sown in a block or a long line is the best way of appreciating the beauty of its tiny flowers.

THYME TO EDGE YOUR GARDEN

Thyme is the ideal garden edging plant. It likes the dryness and sunniness of the border of the garden; it is low growing and not invasive and whenever you kneel on the edge of the garden to pull up a weed you'll get the scent of thyme.

Thyme Quiche

4 SMALL OR 2 LARGE SERVES

~ *2 cups (16 fl oz) cream*

~ *4 eggs, beaten*

~ *1 cup (8 oz) ricotta cheese*

~ *1 tbspn fresh thyme*

Mix all the ingredients together. Pour into an uncooked pastry shell. Preheat oven to 180°C (350°F). Bake until the filling is just set (about 30 minutes).

Thyme and Anchovy Pizza

MAKES A 'MEDIUM' SIZED
PIZZA — 1 LARGE OR 4
SMALL SERVES

CRUST:

~ 5 cups (20 oz) plain (all-
purpose) flour

~ 1 sachet dried (powdered)
yeast

TOPPING:

~ 3 Spanish onions, chopped

~ olive oil

~ 1 cup (5 oz) whole black
olives

~ 1 small can anchovies

~ a generous sprinkling of fresh
thyme

Preheat the oven to 230°C
(450°F).
Mix the flour and yeast and
add enough water to moisten the
dough without making it sticky.
Knead well, spread it on to a
medium pizza tray and leave to
rise for 10 minutes.
Meanwhile, sauté the onions in
the olive oil until transparent.
Cover the pizza dough with the
topping ingredients. Bake in the
preheated oven until the outside
of the crust is brown. Serve hot.

DRIED THYME

Although I don't recommend dried thyme for cooking — not if you've got fresh thyme — any thyme is better than no thyme at all, though I admit that the flavour of dried thyme survives much better than most other herbs. If you have to buy thyme, remember that the more powdery the leaves, the older the herb is and the less fragrance it will have. Old herbs not only lose their strength they lose much of their subtle 'under flavours' as well.

Never buy large quantities of dried thyme — thyme is delicious, but not something you want to pass on to your grandchildren. Try to buy your herbs from a shop with a large turnover; packets of dried herbs sometimes sit on the shelves for a year or more till sold. Once the packet is opened, store it in a sealed glass jar, and throw it away once the fresh flavour has gone. It's no use spoiling a dish just to save a pittance on herbs. Stale herbs spoil a dish. It's better to leave them out or substitute other fresh ones — or use another recipe — than to use what can smell like powdered compost.

24
~

How to Dry Thyme

Thyme has its best flavour when in flower. Cut thyme in the early morning when the dew has dried but the sun still isn't at full strength. By mid-afternoon the thyme may be slightly wilted, or a little of the fragrant oil might have evaporated.

Bunch the thyme stalks into small posies and tie them with a string or ribbon. Hang them in a dark, breezy place — the doorway of a spare room is excellent, if the door isn't opened often and the blinds are kept shut. If the spot isn't airy the leaves may rot; if it is too light or hot the leaves may fade or drop or lose their fragrance. When the leaves are quite dry, hang them in their permanent place.

Bunches of dried thyme are green and fragrant. They are lovely tied above the stove to release their fragrance in the steamy warmth or arranged with fresh flowers in small vases through winter. Thyme can also be rubbed off its stalks once it is dry and placed in a dry jar with the lid firmly secured.

You can take major cuttings of thyme at least once a year, and at least twice for well established bushes.

SERVES 4

This is wonderful — don't condemn it before you have tried it, in spite of the odd combination of flavours. The strawberries must be fragrant — if you can't smell them at arm's length, don't bother with them. And the orange juice must be freshly squeezed. The recipe won't be a success with elderly or commercial orange juice.

~ *1 kg (2 lb) very ripe, firm, fragrant strawberries*
~ *1 cup (8 fl oz) olive oil*
~ *½ cup (4 fl oz) freshly squeezed orange juice*
~ *a generous grind of fresh black pepper*
~ *10 sprigs fresh lemon thyme*

Mix all the ingredients together and leave for 30 minutes in a cool place. Don't chill the strawberries or the sweetness will be lost. Serve with hunks of brie or a mozzarella-type cheese.

Thyme Butter

~ *1 part thyme leaves, stripped from the stalk*
~ *3 parts butter*

Mash the two together, place in small pots and cover with plastic wrap. These will keep for a month in the refrigerator.

Thyme Oil

Thyme can be covered with olive oil, or any bland oil, and preserved for a year or more. I don't recommend this as other herbs make better fragrant oils and thyme loses its fervour and freshness and becomes rubbery in oil. The oil itself is delicious in salads, but a few fresh thyme leaves tossed in at the last moment are even better.

Thyme Ice

Thyme ice blocks are lovely in summer soups. Use them instead of plain ice blocks in Gaspacho or Cold Potato Soup.

Mix 1 part thyme leaves with 20 parts of water. Freeze in an ice-block tray.

USING DRIED THYME

While fresh thyme is best added towards the end of cooking, dried thyme is best added near the beginning. This allows the slightly tough leaves to dissolve and the flavour to permeate. Dried thyme is best used in dishes that require long, slow cooking; the longer and slower they are cooked, the less taste difference from fresh thyme. Dried thyme in an oxtail stew, cooked over two days, will be almost indistinguishable from fresh thyme, as will dried thyme used as stuffing for a slow-cooked shoulder of lamb.

Use slightly less than half the quantity you would normally use of fresh thyme. Dried thyme is not only stronger, it is harsher, and can swamp a dish. Use with discretion.

WHICH THYME TO USE

THYME AFTER THYME

Thyme can most conveniently be categorised for garden use into two groups — clumping kitchen thyme, of which *Thymus vulgaris* is the most common — and matting thyme, of which the most well known is probably *Thymus serpyllum*. Clumping thymes are usually more fragrant than matting thymes, and richer in thymol, one of thyme's essential oils. They are also the most commonly used thymes for perfume, cosmetics and medicines.

Matting thymes are also fragrant, though they are usually not as richly perfumed, and can also be used wherever clumping thymes are used, though the effect won't be as strong. Matting thymes are perfect for thyme lawns, thyme walls, thyme seats and to use between paving stones.

The following thymes are all commercially available. Once you start collecting thymes you come to realise that the genealogy of many thymes is confused, and even named nursery varieties may not be what they seem. The hybridisation and places of origin of thyme fill many pages of argument among thyme experts. If in doubt, sniff and taste.

Simple Gaspacho

~ 4 cups (32 fl oz) tomato juice
~ 2 squashy red tomatoes, peeled and chopped
~ 4 cloves garlic, finely chopped
~ 1 cucumber, chopped
~ chives, chopped, or a very small amount of Spanish onion (so finely chopped it's almost shaved)

Mix all the ingredients together. Place two thyme ice blocks in each bowl.

Cold Potato Soup with Thyme Ice blocks

~ 500 g (1 lb) potatoes
~ 1 cup (8 fl oz) cream
~ juice of 2 lemons
~ 3 cups (24 fl oz) chicken stock, defatted
~ chives, chopped

Boil and mash the potatoes. Add the remaining ingredients and mix well. Cool. To serve, place 2 thyme ice blocks in each bowl.

Clumping Culinary Thymes

Kitchen Thyme (Thymus vulgaris)

This is the best known of all thymes, the classic culinary thyme. It is native to the western Mediterranean region and northern Italy and can still be found wild but is cultivated over most of the world. In many parts of Europe it has become wild since it was introduced.

Thymus vulgaris grows to 40 cm (16 in) high. It flowers in summer, with small two-lipped whitish to pale purple flowers, followed by small fruit, though these are so small that the kitchen gardener is usually unaware of them.

There are several cultivars of kitchen thyme available. Some are hardier or more fragrant than others. Plant kitchen thyme at any time of the year, as long as the ground isn't frozen. It can be grown from seed (kitchen thyme grows relatively true to type) or cuttings.

Kitchen thyme is best kept clipped or it becomes woody. The new leaves grow further and further out from the main stem, and the stem itself tends to break down. The bush then looks ugly and is vulnerable to dieback. I try to cut my thyme bushes back every winter but if you have only a couple of bushes regular use will keep them trimmed. Don't try to cut back thyme bushes too severely at any one time. This can also cause dieback. (See the section on Revitalising Thyme Bushes.)

Orange Thyme (Thymus vulgaris *var.* fragrantissimus)

There is also at least one orange-scented matting thyme. The bush form of orange thyme has narrow grey-green leaves and pale purple flowers. It forms a neat bush about the same height as *Thymus vulgaris* — about 30.5 cm (12 in). The leaves have a distinct citrus scent, quite different from lemon thyme, though perhaps not strongly orange scented either.

Silver Thyme (Thymus argenteus)

This is a mounding thyme, rather than a bushy one. Its leaves are variegated bright green and yellow-white. The whole plant looks silver from a distance. Our silver thyme isn't quite as fragrant as other thymes, though it might simply be a poor specimen. Some catalogues list silver thyme as a lemon thyme, but I have yet to smell one that gives a whiff of citrus.

Silver thyme will do well in partial shade, especially late afternoon shade, and won't do well in exposed situations. It needs slightly more water than common thyme, though it is still a hardy plant.

Cone Head Thyme (Thymus capitatus)

This is one of the main thymes used to extract thymol from the leaves and flowers, for use in cosmetics, perfumery and liqueurs.

Lemon Thyme (Thymus x citriodorus)

Lemon thyme is intermediate between matting and clumping thyme. It forms a low long bush rather than a woody one, but doesn't form a mat either. Lemon thyme and its derivatives are not wild thymes but deliberate cultivars, with strongly scented leaves that are excellent in cooking. The flowers are pale lilac, appearing from mid to late summer. *Thymus* x *citriodorus* is best grown from cuttings, as seedlings may not grow true to type.

Variegated Lemon Thyme

Thymed Mushroom Salad

SERVES 4

~ 500 g (1 lb) fresh mushrooms, sliced
~ 1 tbspn fresh thyme
~ 1 red capsicum (sweet pepper), finely sliced
~ ½ stick celery, very finely sliced
~ 3 cloves garlic, chopped

DRESSING:

~ 1 part fresh lime juice (use lemon, if you must)
~ 4 parts olive oil
~ plenty of freshly ground black pepper
~ salt (optional)

Combine all the salad ingredients. Add the dressing and toss lightly. Serve cold. This is good served immediately; it is more rubbery but also more fragrant served after marinating for a couple of hours.

An alternative is to sauté all the ingredients except the lemon juice in the olive oil; add the lemon juice right at the end. Serve hot.

Thymed Tomatoes

❧

SERVES 2–4

~ 4 ripe tomatoes

~ 1 cup (8 fl oz) cream

~ 1 tbspn fresh thyme

~ 6 cloves garlic, chopped

Immerse the tomatoes in boiling water for a few seconds to remove the skins.

Pour into a frying pan the cream, thyme and garlic. Simmer for 10 minutes. Add the tomatoes. Simmer just long enough to heat the tomatoes through — they shouldn't begin to get mushy. Serve at once. The cream will have thickened slightly into a herb-rich sauce.

Silver queen (Thymus citriodorus 'Silver Queen') is a silver-leaved lemon thyme cultivar, though it can vary considerably in its appearance. It flowers in summer and needs a cooler, moister spot than common lemon thyme.

Golden lemon thyme (Thymus citriodorus aureus) is a golden-leaved variety of lemon thyme. The fragrance is as strong but the leaves are rich yellow. To some people golden leaves are striking; to others they look like a nutrient deficiency. It is smaller than the green version, with a slightly more creeping habit. Green and yellow thymes can be alternated if you like patchwork herb gardens.

Spanish Thyme (Thymus mastichina)

This is another grey-foliaged thyme. It is one of the neatest thymes, forming a rounded clump, though like all thymes it responds best to regular trimming. It has a classic thyme fragrance, sweet and strong, and is an excellent cooking thyme. It is used in Spain for flavouring olives.

Silver Posie Thyme (Thymus serpyllum 'Silver Posie')

An ornamental thyme, very low growing, though not as flat as a matting thyme. It forms an attractive clump and doesn't die back from the middle as much as common thyme does. It will tolerate more shade than common thyme and, conversely, won't take the extremes of heat and dryness that common thyme thrives on. Silver posie thyme leaves are bright green with silver edges and the scent is strongly herbal, rather than a classic thyme perfume. It can be used in cooking but is better if used with discretion, and not where a classic thyme taste is expected.

Westmoreland or Turkey Thyme (Thymus westmoreland)
This is an incredibly fragrant thyme, and one of the best for cooking. It is also one of the most attractive thymes being a rich deep green with a larger leaf than common thyme.

Westmoreland thyme makes a very low bush, almost a mat, and is fast growing — one bush will provide enough leaves even for quite avid thyme users. Its pale purple flowers are also fragrant (though admittedly you have to bend down a long way to smell them, unless you can sit on a bank above them where the scent will float up to you). Westmoreland thyme is one of the earliest thymes to flower, in late spring.

Thymus Vulgaris

*Zucchini (Courgettes)
and Tomatoes with
Lemon Thyme*

SERVES 2–4

~ 4 ripe tomatoes
~ 6 small zucchini, chopped
~ 6 cloves garlic, chopped
~ ½ cup (4 fl oz) olive oil
~ 1 tbspn red wine vinegar
~ 1 tsp lemon thyme leaves

*Skin the tomatoes by
immersing them in boiling
water for a few seconds, then
chop them.
Sauté the zucchini and garlic
in the olive oil. When the
zucchini are slightly brown,
add the chopped tomatoes. As
soon as the tomatoes start to
ooze, add the vinegar and
thyme. Serve hot.*

Cat Thyme

MATTING THYMES
(*THYMUS SERPYLLUM, THYMUS PRAECOX*
AND A CONFUSION AND PROFUSION OF
OTHERS)

Creeping thyme, wild thyme, matting thyme

This has the charming nickname of 'mother of
thymes'. It is a 'wild' thyme (though of course all
but the recently bred thymes were once wild). It
is found over much of Europe and Asia and as far
north as Iceland.

Wild thyme is very variable and has numerous
wild and garden cultivars, all differing in leaf
size, colour and growth habits. Generally,
though, all are fast growing, extremely prostrate
and mat forming and all make excellent thyme
lawns or wall edging. The flowers are pale pink to
purple, from late summer to autumn.

Thymus serpyllum is sometimes called
'Shakespeare's thyme', but it probably isn't.

Cat Thyme (Teucrium marum)

Though not a true thyme, this small grey-leaved matting plant is often included in lists of thymes and looks just like one to the casual observer. It has thyme-shaped leaves with a faint though pungent scent, said to be irresistible to cats. I've found that the wild cats either ignore it or sniff round it, fascinated — it depends on the cat. Try cat thyme as a present for your domestic cat, or to keep neighbours pets away from your seedlings — just plant a patch of cat thyme in an area you don't mind them visiting. We use our patch to lure the feral cats, so we can trap them, to stop them decimating the wild birds.

Cat thyme appears to grow more slowly than most matting thymes. It needs full sun and won't tolerate wet soil so keep it away from moisture-loving plants. Prune a little after flowering to encourage new growth. It is another good plant for the rockery — as long as you don't mind cats on your rockery as well.

Red-flowered thyme (Thymus coccineus)

This is a red-flowered matting thyme. The flowers are the deepest coloured of all the thyme flowers and are shown to advantage against dark green leaves.

Caraway Thyme (Thymus herba-barona)

A small-leaved matting thyme from Corsica, strongly caraway scented. It gets its name from its use in cooking barons of beef. It has reddish-purple flowers. I have found it slow to establish, but when growing well the caraway scent will rise around you on a hot, still day. It is an

Chicken with Prunes and Thyme

SERVES 4

~ 1 kg (2 lb) chicken pieces, pressed into a little cornflour to remove moisture
~ 2 slices bacon, chopped
~ 6 tbspns olive oil
~ 1 cup (8 fl oz) white wine
~ ½ cup (3 oz) pitted prunes
~ 1 cup (8 fl oz) water or chicken stock
~ 1 cup (8 fl oz) cream
~ 1 tsp fresh thyme

Sauté the chicken and bacon in the olive oil until the chicken is brown. Remove the chicken and add the white wine. Reduce until the chicken and bacon bits are combined with the liquid. Place the browned chicken pieces and the liquid, together with the prunes and water or stock, into a large casserole with a heavy lid.

Cook in a slow oven (170°C/300°F) for 1 hour. Remove from the oven. Take out the chicken and prunes and add the cream and thyme to the sauce. Let it bubble till it thickens. Return the chicken and prunes to the casserole and cook till the joints are no longer pink — anywhere from 5 to 20 minutes. Don't overcook the chicken or it will be stringy.

Rabbit with Apple, Calvados and Lemon Thyme

~ 1 rabbit, jointed

~ 3–4 tbspns olive oil

~ 1–3 tbspns calvados

~ 1 cup (8 fl oz) cream

~ 2 tart (Granny Smith) apples, peeled and sliced

~ 1 tspn fresh thyme

Brown the jointed rabbit in the olive oil. Place the joints in a casserole. Add the calvados to the pan in which you browned the meat, and allow to bubble till reduced by half. Scrape the mixture into the casserole with the rabbit. Now add the cream, the apples, and the lemon thyme. Cook in a very slow oven (170°C/300°F) till the rabbit is tender, the apple almost dissolved, and the sauce becomes very thick.

excellent herb to plant in paving, and the stored heat seems to bring out the scent.

Caraway thyme is a very hardy variety for exposed spots like the tops of walls or rockeries. It is perhaps the least shade tolerant of the common thymes and dies back very rapidly if it doesn't have full sun and a light, dryish soil. It also makes a far less dense mat than most of the other matting thymes and so is not really suitable for a lawn. Even though this is not considered a pretty thyme — the leaves are dull and small and pointed — its wonderful fragrance more than compensates.

Parsley Thyme (Thymus integer)

A green matting thyme with a fresh parsley scent. It is softer than most matting thymes and forms a dense sward. It needs some protection from very heavy frost, as well as relatively moist soil.

Grey Woolly Thyme (Thymus laniginosa)

Grey carpets can be very restful in a colourful garden, and grey woolly thyme has a soft appeal of its own. *Thymus lanuginosus* is a furry grey-leaved thyme, with pale purple-pink flowers. It is a reasonably rapid grower — the more sun the faster it grows. It flowers in summer and bears its flowers on relatively long stems.

34
~

Thymus nitidus

A small, shrubby thyme with blue-grey leaves and pale pinkish lavender flowers. It forms gentle mounds rather than a flat mat or woody clumps. It is taller and wider than most clumps of thyme and can spread to almost 100 cm (39 in). It is an excellent thyme to let ramble down a bank, or from a tall pot. Unlike most matting thymes the fragrance isn't classic thyme but has a hint of orange and rosemary or spice as well.

Lemon Matting Thyme (Thymus pulegoides)

This has a strong lemon thyme scent like the culinary lemon thyme, though its small leaves are harder to pick, and it is not as fast growing.

Doone Valley Thyme

This may be a variegated form of lemon-scented *Thymus pulegoides*, with reddish purple flowers in midsummer. The young leaves on the top of new shoots are dark green with gold markings, though they can turn rusty after frost. The older leaves remain green. Doone Valley is faintly lemon scented but can be used for cooking, though other thymes are better if you have them.

Doone Valley can be damaged by heavy frost, usually towards the centre of the plant. A movable cold frame will give some protection. (See the section on Revitalising Thyme Bushes). Doone Valley does best in a sheltered, though sunny, spot and needs more moisture than most matting thymes.

Thymus Laniginosa

This was my favourite dish at
my grandmother's. It is
English cooking at its best.

~ *1 onion, chopped*

~ *3 tbspns butter*

~ *1 cup (2 oz) soft*
breadcrumbs

~ *1 tbspn fresh thyme (either*
kitchen thyme or lemon thyme)

~ *2 sage leaves, chopped*

~ *1 egg*

~ *1 shoulder of lamb or*
mutton

Sauté the onion in the butter
until the onion is transparent.
Mix with the rest of the
stuffing ingredients.

   Cut a long, deep slice next to
the bone in the shoulder of
lamb or mutton (mutton or
'two tooth' is better and has
more flavour but it's hard to
find these days). Insert the
stuffing. Roast the lamb very,
very slowly with potatoes,
pumpkin, parsnips and carrots
around it.

White-flowered Thyme
(Thymus serpyllum albus)

This is a white-flowered version of wild thyme, fairly low growing, and the leaves are much more rounded than most thymes. White thyme is the last thyme to flower each summer.

Golden Thyme (Thymus serpyllum aureum)

A bright gold mat with purple flowers.

Annie Hall (Thymus sp.)

This is another white-flowered matting thyme. It has incredibly small, light green leaves. It is slow growing but forms a very dense carpet, though like all thymes it can die back with too much moisture. It has very small white to pale pink flowers, and in midsummer these can completely

Thymus Herba-barona

shade out the leaves. Even so, it cannot be called a spectacular flowerer as the flowers are much the same shade as the leaves, and both are tiny.

Lars Hall (Thymus *sp.*)
This has pink flowers.

Magic Carpet (Thymus *sp.*)
A fast growing thyme, with deep pink flowers.

Pink Chintz (Thymus *sp.*)
Pink chintz is a pink-flowered thyme, fast growing and adaptable. It is very aptly named — the grey-green foliage and the dusty pink flowers are very like a chintz fabric.

Thyme-Flavoured Barbecued Chops or Chicken

Just before you place the meat on the barbecue, throw some branches of thyme onto the coals. They release their fragrance immediately and impart it to the meat. Don't bother trying this with sausages — the skins are too tough for the flavour to penetrate.

37
~

THYME AS A COMPANION PLANT

Thyme is an excellent companion for cucumbers — just slip the cucumber seeds next to the thyme plants. The thyme flowers will attract bees to pollinate the cucumber flowers (some modern cucumber cultivars are not very attractive to bees, and fruit set can be poor). The thyme also appears to inhibit powdery mildew. Make sure you stake the cucumbers, otherwise the leaves will cover the thyme and make them susceptible to disease.

Carpets of thyme between your summer-flowering fruit trees or shrubs will keep thrips on the flowers at ground level and away from the flowers on your trees. (Don't grow thyme directly under fruit trees — thyme doesn't like the shade. A strip of thyme between the trees, however, works well.)

Thyme planted near cabbages, broccoli, etc. is said to deter cabbage root fly (I haven't tried this; it may be folklore). Thyme is also supposed to help keep away cabbage white butterflies. I have tested this; it didn't work.

A strong 'thyme tea' may help keep away those pests that are attracted to their food source by scent, though usually other deterrents will also be needed.

MEDICINAL THYME

It helpest against the bitings of any venomous beast either taken in drink or outwardly applied

~

THE ELIZABETHAN HERBALIST, JOHN GERARD (1545–   )

According to the medieval herbalist Dr Culpeper (Culpeper was a famous but not terribly expert herbalist who had his detractors even in his own time) ... *thyme ... being a notable herb of Venus, provokes the terms, gives safe and speedy delivery to women in travail, and brings away the afterbirth. An ointment of it takes away hot swellings and warts, helps the sciatica and dullness of sight, and takes away pains and hardness of the spleen. It is exellent for those troubled with the gout; as also, to annoint the testicles that are swelled ... the herb taken inwardly ... expels wind.*
Wild thyme, according to Culpeper, was a sure remedy for nightmares.

Thyme has a long history of medicinal use. It was used by the ancient Egyptians as part of the embalming process for the dead. It was one of the ancient incense herbs and one of the medieval strewing herbs. (Herbs were strewn on the floor with rushes to help keep away fleas and other pests, as well as to sweeten the fairly putrid medieval halls.) It was also mentioned by the Greek physician Dioscorides in *De Materia Medica*, which became the standard reference work for 1500 years.

Thymol, one of thyme's essential oils, is an extremely powerful antiseptic, used in several commercial mouthwashes, toothpastes and

*Thyme Mouth Wash
(for gum infections
or sore throat)*

✿➳

Add 100 g (3½ oz) of dried
thyme to 4 cups (32 fl oz) of
hot water. Leave till cold.
Gargle at least three times a
day.

*Tincture of Thyme for
Athlete's Foot or to Kill
Nits*

✿➳

Cover 100 g (3½ oz) of dried
thyme with 2 cups
(16 fl oz) brandy. Keep in a
sealed jar and shake every day
for two weeks. This tincture
may be made with vinegar
instead, but isn't as effective.
It can also be made with rum,
brandy or any other alcohol.
Apply once a day for athlete's
foot; or leave overnight for nits
and reapply 10 days later.

gargles. Thyme has also been used to kill
intestinal worms, for urinary tract infections, and
to disinfect wounds.

While most of thyme's medicinal applications
need the advice of a qualified practitioner, you
might care to try some of the following.

THYME AND LOW SALT DIETS

If you are trying to convert to a low salt diet,
thyme will give the impression of added salt.

THYME AND ANIMALS

Thyme used to be given to sheep and goats to
increase their milk yield. (I don't know if this
works or not.) It was also given to domestic stock,
including hens, to rid them of worms. Equal
parts of thyme were mixed with a hot bran mash
and fed to the hens in the morning.

DRINKING THYME

Thyme is used as the base for many traditional drinks, including Benedictine and Chartreuse. It was a more common ingredient in medieval drinks than it is today — one of many wild ingredients in a production of herb beers, herb tonics and herbal tisanes.

Carl Linnaeus, one of the founders of modern systematic botany, recommended thyme as a cure for a hangover.

A Modern Version of Medieval Metheglin

(Note: This is not recommended for modern palates. Most medieval dishes are far too highly flavoured for today's taste.)

Take a handful of violet leaves, strawberry leaves, 2 handfuls of violet flowers and rose hips, a handful of thyme leaves, a pinch of rosemary and coriander seeds. Cover with 2 litres of water. Simmer for 20 minutes; strain; add ½ cup of honey and a pinch of dried yeast when tepid. (The dried yeast would have been ale barm.) When the mixture is fermenting nicely add a grate of nutmeg, 2 cloves and a dust of cinnamon.

Place it in a container with an airlock; bottle it when the fermentation stops. It should be ready in 6 months, and does not improve with keeping.

Thyme Cough Mixture

~ 1 tbspn thyme

~ 1 tbspn coltsfoot leaves

~ 1 tbspn horehound leaves

~ 1 tbspn anise seed

~ 1 tbspn honey

~ 2 cups (16 fl oz) boiling water

Mix all the ingredients together. Leave till cool; reheat and sip as necessary.

Thyme Bath

This is said to ease rheumatic pain. Take a bunch of dried thyme tied securely at the stalk (so the thyme doesn't spread all over the bath and make it look like a vegetable stew). Place the thyme under the hot tap as you run the bath. The volatile oil is said to be absorbed by the skin; and by inhalation as the steam rises.

A Thyme Remedy for Baldness

(This doesn't work. Give it to Uncle Harry for Christmas.)

Cover 1 tbspn of dried thyme with 1 cup (8 fl oz) of hot water. Leave till cold. Use to rinse the hair once a day.

Thyme Cold Reliever

Thyme helps soothe sore throats, loosens mucus and relieves inflammation due to coughing.

~ *1 tbspn dried thyme*

~ *1 tbspn honey*

~ *1 cup (8 fl oz) hot water*

Combine all the ingredients and leave till cool. Strain. Reheat to blood heat, and sip.

THYME COSMETICS

Thyme Cleanser for Oily Skin

2 tbspns rolled oats

1 tsp cornflour

2 tbspns milk

liquid from 1 tbspn thyme soaked in 3 tbspns boiling water

Heat all ingredients gently till the mixture begins to thicken. Cool, and smooth a thin layer over your skin. Leave it for 10 minutes before washing off.

Thyme Footbath (to freshen the feet)

Heat 2 cups (16 fl oz) water with ½ cup (4 fl oz) cider vinegar and 2 tbspns thyme; simmer 5 minutes. Cool till just bearable, then insert the feet. Leave till the footbath is cool, then dry the feet well.

Thyme Hair Rinse

Heat 1 cup (8 fl oz) cider vinegar with 2 cups (16 fl oz) water and 1 tbspn thyme. Simmer 2 minutes. Cool and bottle. Use a little to rinse your hair to remove the soap residue and leave it shining and fragrant.

Herbal Bathbag

The scent of thyme in this bag is said to be invigorating. The combination of oats and thyme helps cleanse the skin, and certainly seems to soften it.

Combine 3 tbspns of dried thyme with 2 cups (6 oz) of rolled (not instant) oats. Sew into a small bag made from old towelling or a sheet, or any attractive, colour-fast cloth. Use this 'herbal sponge' in the bath or shower. It will last about a week.

GIFTS FROM THYME

THYME HONEY

The bees alluring thyme

~

SPENSER

Thyme honey is a Mediterranean delicacy — beehives are kept in
pastures of cultivated thyme, or moved to hillsides of wild thyme in
midsummer.

Thyme honey is dark and very strongly scented. It sounds wonderfully
romantic and has been appreciated by gourmets for over two thousand
years. But to be honest, I would rather taste my thyme and honey
separately — thyme honey overpowers everything it's eaten with, and
to my mind tastes like mouthwash. But we keep beehives, and when
the bees browse among the thyme as well as the eucalyptus blossom, a
touch of thyme honey gives a subtle depth to an otherwise bland
vintage.

A THYME GARLAND

*Use as an accompaniment to
cold meat, especially chicken,
or with hot pork.*

~ *1 cup (8 fl oz) clear apple
juice*

~ *1 cup (8 fl oz) chicken stock*

~ *2 tbspns gelatine dissolved
in a little hot water. (If you
are using good home-made
clarified stock you won't need
gelatine)*

~ *1 tbspn fresh thyme leaves,
preferably lemon or orange
thyme*

~ *1 tsp very finely chopped
chives*

*Combine the apple juice and
chicken stock. Heat gently then
add the gelatine, thyme and
chives. Pour into small, clear
jars; secure the lids. Keep the
jellies in the refrigerator until
needed, though they will
survive a day or so out of the
refrigerator in a cool place.*

Take long strips of willow branch and twist them
to form a wreath shape. (Fuse wire can be used
instead.) Twist sprigs of flowering thyme through
the wire or willow until all the infrastructure is
covered. Intertwine a few daisies or other small
flowers, or sprigs of other herbs, or intertwine
ribbons for colour. Hang the thyme garland by a
window so the sunlight will draw out the
fragrance.

A Thyme and Garlic Ribbon

This is for the nimble fingered.
Take fresh garlic, still with its long leaves and
stems attached. Plait them together, intertwining
their long leaves with small stalks of flowering
thyme. More accurate directions than this
probably won't help — it's a matter of letting
your fingers find the way. Once the ribbon is
complete you can also sew small chillies onto the
garlic leaves to add colour.
Hang the thyme and garlic ribbons above the
stove or give them as gifts.

Thyme Potpourri

*Most potpourris are sweet and
floral. This one is spicy and
fragrant. It will freshen a
room without being cloying.*

*Mix together 1 cup thyme
leaves, with stalks attached,
the grated rind of 1 orange
and 1 lemon and 1 cup mint
leaves.*

*Leave the thyme, grated rind
and mint on newspaper in the
sun for a day. They should be
almost dry — rubbery but not
crunchy. Mix with 2 tbspns of
orris root, or 1 cup cistus
leaves (either of these will 'fix'
the perfume so the scent lasts
longer).*

*Place a bowl of thyme
potpourri near the doorway, or
near a window where the heat
will release the scent.*

*If your potpourri is fading,
a few drops of brandy dribbled
on the leaves will freshen it
again.*

THYME POSIES

Thyme Moth Repellent

Mix together equal
quantities of dried thyme,
dried wormwood, dried tansy
and dried cloves. Seal into
sachets.

Thyme Incense

Mix 1 cup grated orange peel
with 1 cup thyme leaves and
twigs and add a stick of
cinnamon.
Leave in the sun on sheets of
newspaper until completely
dry. Pound in a mortar till
roughly combined then add a
little saltpetre. Pile the incense
in a pyramid shape and set
alight. This should ward off
the bubonic plague!

Thyme is such a small bush that it is easy to
overlook the flowers. This is a pity as they are
charming — and a small posy has the advantage
of fragrant leaves as well as pretty flowers.
Pick the flowers and place them in nosegay vases,
or decorative eggcups, on the table — one to each
place setting if possible. Thyme flowers are best
combined with other small flowers like alyssum,
miniature roses, or tiny daisies.

46
~

AND FINALLY ...
A SIMPLE THYME SPELL

Thick growing thyme, and roses wet with dew
Are sacred to the sisterhood divine.

~

ANONYMOUS ENGLISH POET (1799)

Most common wild herbs have been ascribed with some magic power in the past, partly because witches, like herbalists and all great chefs, worked with what was available around them.

Thyme was one of the fairy herbs. The king of the fairies and his court were said to dance on banks of wild thyme on midsummer night's eve. (Maybe they still do.) I don't know if this was because of any magic effect of thyme. Perhaps they just liked the fragrance.

Thyme used in the following way is supposed to increase strength, awareness and courage. (Note: I haven't tried this recipe, and in no way vouch for its effectiveness.)

Fill the bath at dusk with hot, pure water. This should be spring water, not city tap water (I doubt that chemicals are any help to spells), though you may have to risk the city water. Light the bathroom with candles. Don't turn on the light. Throw in 3 cups of thyme leaves.

Bathe in the water until it cools, concentrating on the scent of thyme. According to medieval medical lore, if the magic fails and this doesn't fill you with strength or courage, it may do wonders for your rheumatism. It may also help your tinea.

ACKNOWLEDGMENTS

The publisher would like to thank Dr R.W. Lyndon for the use of his garden at McMahons Point and the following organisations in New South Wales, Australia, for kindly supplying various photographic props:

The Grosvenor Antique Centre, Lindfield

Appley Hoare Antiques, Woollahra

Home & Garden on the Mall, Sky Gardens

Wild Australia, Sky Gardens

Swane's Nursery, Dural

Garden & Pool Essentials, Roseville

Sweet Violets, Lindfield

~ ~ ~

PHOTOGRAPHY
Scott Cameron Photography Pty Ltd

FOOD STYLIST
Lisa Hilton

ILLUSTRATION
Dianne Bradley

COVER PHOTOGRAPHY
Ivy Hansen